OR WHERE A YOUNG PENGUI

OR WHERE A YOUNG PENGUIN LIES SCREAMING

POEMS

by

GAVIN EWART

LONDON . VICTOR GOLLANCZ LTD . 1979

First published February 1978
Second impression June 1978
Third impression June 1979

ISBN 0 575 02342 2

ACKNOWLEDGEMENTS

Some of these poems have appeared in: *Ambit, Encounter, The Honest Ulsterman, London Magazine, The Listener, The Little Word Machine, The New Review, The New Statesman, The Times Literary Supplement.*

'Home Truths' appeared in *New Poetry 1* and 'Oh, Darling!' in *New Poetry 2* (the Arts Council anthologies). 'Shakespeare' was written for the Poems For Shakespeare programme organized by Sam Wanamaker at the Globe Playhouse. 'A Wee Sang For St. Andrew's Day' was included in *Twelve Apostles*, a pamphlet published by *The Honest Ulsterman*.

In Section 3, there are some semantic poems, or synonymic poems. Semantic poetry, properly speaking (where dictionary definitions replace the main nouns, verbs and adjectives) was invented by Stefan Themerson in his brilliant novel *Bayamus*.

PRINTED PHOTOLITHO IN GREAT BRITAIN
BY EBENEZER BAYLIS AND SON, LTD.
THE TRINITY PRESS, WORCESTER, AND LONDON

For Lincoln Kirstein

Someone who laughs
Has merely not yet heard
The appalling news.
                    —Bertold Brecht tr. David Craig

I've often said to meself, I've said
"Cheer up, cully, you'll soon be dead"
                    —*The Arcadians*

Would you rather live in peaceful Putney
or where a young penguin lies screaming?

Would you rather live in wonderful Wandsworth
or where a young penguin lies screaming?

Would you rather live in lively London
or where a young penguin lies screaming?

CONTENTS

Section 1

THE GENTLE SEX (1974)

On Tuesday, 23rd July,
   in that black sectarian Belfast
under a rainy, cramped and hopeless sky
   five Loyalist women at last,
after a false alarm visit the previous day,
found Anne Ogilby in her home; under overcast
   weather, in a little car, they drove her away,
leaving behind her five-year-old daughter Sharlene, who could
                                         only scream and cry.

   Leader of the Women's UDA,
      Lilly Douglas was in charge.
For questioning, to hear what Anne had to say
   (for cloudy suspicions were looming large
over the little terraced houses of Sandy Row,
   full of memories of unemployment and bread and marge)
   why food parcel money, that by rights should go
on food for her boyfriend in Long Kesh, had gone (they
                                         claimed) astray.

      Each month £10.
      One of the women accusing,
   who hunted her down, we could say, like hounds,
      found it far from amusing
that her husband was the boyfriend who had lived with Anne
for a full three months before arrest, refusing
   to return home, father of Anne's baby, a man
who had had enough of her and her marital life—that's how it
                                         sounds.

      They drove to a Loyalist club
      and questioned her, hard and mean;
   but then a UDA man from a pub
      happened to intervene—

this was lucky for her indeed, and it certainly fell
out luckily that he should have come on the scene.
    At a bus station by the Europa Hotel
they left her, released; as scared cats leave birds and dive
                                              under a shrub.

        A dark 31-year-old,
        unmarried mother of four;
    and even a British soldier, the women told,
        was father of one, a whore
    they couldn't call her, pots don't call kettles black,
    but they also said, and protested, a very great deal more
        about betrayed gunmen; a Protestant murder attack
she had witnessed, and the 'kneecapping' of a sheep that
                                          tried to leave the fold.

        Just after 10.15
        Lilly Douglas's teenage daughter
    and another girl, only sixteen,
        stood in front of her bus and caught her.
    They dragged her off. In a small red Fiat, nine
    women started off to a 'Romper Room' in that quarter
        where their traitors are disciplined—fine
for the beaters-up but for the others the fun isn't so good and
                                                      clean.

        But, before they arrived, the car
        was stopped by police, who took
    them all back to the bus station; so far
        no crime—so whom could they book?
    Anne, the police say, kept nervously biting her nails
    but refused to make a complaint (though she did look
        like someone in need of help). Law fails
always where the community knows, and won't tell, who the
                                              killers are.

14

At 10.30, then, next day
(home in the small hours) she
failed to attend at the Welfare; but they
know she was there at three.
Meanwhile, in the Elm Bar, a 'heavy squad' was drinking—
'Bumper' Graham, three unemployed teenage girls. The key
to the whole situation, the woman of action and thinking
was 41-year-old Lilly, smuggler, forger, violent, drunk,
brothel-keeper (police say).

Convicted, too. Gave order:
Graham to fetch Anne from Welfare.
He went. Without force, no lawless marauder,
found her and took her from there.
The welfare officers had not even, then, been seen.
In an Edinburgh hostel, safe in their care,
a place had been found, for both Anne and Sharlene.
This she never knew. Of such missed trains and wrong
destinations Time's a relentless hoarder.

But now: the Romper Room. And,
when Sharlene began to cry,
Graham put 10p into her childish hand,
said she'd see Mammy bye and bye
and told her to go out and buy herself some sweets.
Her mother was blindfolded with a tea towel; we know why
a dark brown bag was put over her head. In the streets
meanwhile life flowed easy in the uneasy city, like the sea
lapping the sand.

Etty Cowan, Chrissie Smith, Joey Brown
wearing, all three, white masks
made from one of Joey's jumpers (put down,
it sounds like a game; but such tasks

come easy in the boredom and poverty of their existence),
walked in and began to 'romper' Anne. Who asks,
      in such circumstances, exactly why? No resistance
was offered as she was pushed and kicked from one to the
                              other—like a circus clown.

            Graham and Joey were upset
         by now. They tried to stop it.
      But Etty Cowan was in her stride, all set,
         took a brick and wouldn't drop it,
      stood over Anne and banged it on her face,
      as hard as she could, a very determined moppet.
         She and Chrissie stopped for a smoke. Some minutes' grace
      she had from that; but soon they began again, giving it all
                              they'd got—or could get.

            Outside the door Sharlene,
         back with a chocolate biscuit, screamed
      (inside, her mother screamed; obscene
         thumps, thuds, gurgles seemed
      the soundtrack of a nightmare, "Mammy, I want my Mammy!'
      echoed outside, a bad dream crudely dreamed),
         through the brown bag perhaps the blood oozed, jammy—
      until she twitched no longer; even for those avengers, the
                              slate wiped clean.

            So when they knew that she'd died
         they went for a bottle of wine.
      They just shooed Sharlene outside
         and onto the streets. The deep mine
      of vengeance was plumbed, the boil lanced.
      The body? Disposed on a motorway. Fine.
         They got into a disco and danced.
      For a good cause, and a mother's jealousy revenged, can make
                              you feel warm inside.

Oedema of the brain,
associated fractures of the skull,
and on the scalp the deepened main
16 separate wounds. Dull
their lives must have been, dull and dull indeed
for this to be their pleasure! The wayward gull
floats over Belfast; animals have no need
for torture. Her face was completely black. And certainly,
chewing gum in court, they'd do it again.

SHAKESPEARE

People facetiously say
your name had you foxed with its spelling;
   and certain it is that the sound

   of your plays was so different from what
reverberates now from our stages
   that we must imagine a blend

   of three accents now oceans apart—
the Dublin, the Cockney, the Boston.
   'Break' was rhyming with 'speak',

   both 'solid' and 'sullied' that flesh,
Falstaff said 'reasons' like 'raisins'
   when he made his blackberry pun,

   there was a mousetrap joke
in 'tropically' spoken by Hamlet.
   Elizabeth even, the Queen,

   that learnèd knitter of speech,
dropped all her aitches like stitches.
   Faucal plosion is all,

   fricatives land on the ear,
and the word is labiodental
   for those who have mastered the craft.

   But accent and dialect, both,
could never obscure your clear meaning—
   a sentence however pronounced

acquits you of being in the power
of the specialist young phonetician.
  Your rhetoric breaks through the net,

  too strong for theory to hold;
and Bernard Shaw said a true thing
  when on the old BBC

  he said that you churned out plays
like a series of cinema scripts that
  were wanted, and fast, for new films;

  a parallel now—better still—
would be with the insatiable telly.
  Repeats were not common, a play

  might be performed once and no more.
Quick-change artistes and clever
  at patching on workable scenes

  all of them had to be then—
tradition alone made them poets,
  something to do with the Greeks

  and the mystical power of the verse
that was used for religious persuasion.
  The song, as they said, of the goat.

  You got up some speed; and some fire
flew out of your breathtaking phrases
  as you blasted your way down the track—

  those multitudinous seas
and aroint thee! and that rump-fed ronyon,
  words that for 10-year-old boys

had power in those earlier schools,
where a highbrow word like aesthetics
   suggested the surgeon's knife

or nothing. We smile, but it's true.
It was bear-baiting then or the cock-fights
   or hearing tempestuous shouts

from the Kings and the Queens and the Knaves
and watching the stage-managed battles.
   A choice; and, as Beecham once said,

the British, a Philistine lot,
don't really care much for music—
   they just like the noise that it makes.

So we were lucky all round,
we got you by chance, a great genius,
   and (Honest Iago my foot!)

you fooled them; they thought you wrote plays—
but all the time they were absorbing
   the highest, most durable Art.

"The lion griefs loped from the shade
And on our knees their muzzles laid,
And Death put down his book"

Don't worry,
poetry won't be as good as that again in a hurry!
New "schools", now,
may regard us as a collection of old fools now,
or wonder
what on earth we saw in it—but, no blunder,
what Bach had
(strict formal beauty), what *The Hunting Of The Snark* had,
corroding
and surreal anxiety, a sense of foreboding,
and, in it
all too, the urgency of the actual historical minute—
these made it
more compelling than the craftsman's ear by which he played it.

Each age, I
submit, has its own particular Journey of the Magi;
they carry
the gifts that alone can truly, faithfully, marry
the ideal
to our hesitating, wavering sense of what is real.
So Auden
threw round the political nasties a sort of cordon,
immunising
us against their infecting presence, and rising,
a champion,
a serious singer, a warner, a Baptist, a Campion
with social
significance (a prophet whose "Woe!" shall

be ignored—as
it always is—no more regarded than Harry Lauder's
brash singing)
came at us like Carroll's Bellman with that bell he was ringing!
Swinburne too
once with the young men at Oxford certainly had his turn—to
be chanted
in evening streets. For some sort of Saviour is wanted.
Dogmatics
are twenty years old, with bats in their belfries and attics,
a top storey
that leans, not to work or moderation, but to death and glory,
new magic—
Auden's wonderful hybrid rose that
crossed the comic with the tragic.

HOME TRUTHS

What the censorious wives,
the ones who throw words like knives,
have never understood
is how it's the hen that pecks—
not the hope of better sex—
makes men leave home for good.

By ravenous sirens misled
into an alien bed?
Not so. The better lay
might be in domestic sheets
and it's not for erotic treats
husbands go on their way.

A truly nasty remark
in the conjugal dark
can act as a potent spur—
he only wants to escape,
in any form or shape,
the flying of the fur.

He longs for a different diet—
a little peace and quiet;
and to be always told
how he's an also-ran
and really hardly a man
makes him feel very old.

The Other Woman waits,
and she's not hurling plates
or thinking him inept

or running a permanent quiz;
it's him, just as he is,
she will accept.

The stir of a woman's tongue
has got some good men hung
in more vindictive days.
Trouble is what it stirs—
not his alone, but hers—
there's death in a phrase.

TRUE LOVE

QUEEN IDDY, musty pusty the fur-faced rat and Daffer Down Dilly send all love to BUM FACE.

GROWLY BEAR, the hedgehog loves you just a tiny tiny little bit.

MARCELLA, compliments of the Season from the Trollyfrog.

DESPERATE DAN loves DORMOUSE for ever and ever.

—Valentine Day Notices, *The Guardian,* 14th February, 1976.

> From the unconscious, look what surfaced:
> a bear, a frog, a rat that's fur-faced!
> That's love for you! Infantile, it
> thinks baby talk's sure to beguile, it
> seriously believes in magic
> (and what reads comic might be tragic)
> where all *tristitia amoris*
> is simplified to fairy stories.
> Love, on this evidence, evinces
> a touching faith in all Frog Princes
> and such anthropomorphic fauna—
> far from our world of sex and sauna,
> which animal spirits don't make frisky
> half as much as tots of whisky.
> MARCELLA's lover, dark and shady,
> might be a Lesbian tea-lady?
> A Trollyfrog? And who's QUEEN IDDY?
> a cute chick or a fat old biddy?
> In lower case, too, musty pusty
> sounds unwholesome, dirty, dusty—

love's trafficking in what's ideal
disguises what's pathetic, real
and subject to the years' bite, foully
ageing, bad-tempered—in short GROWLY.

Bad life, bad sex, bad love not mentioned—
at least such words are well-intentioned,
comforting (though not too clever), land
us in a lovely Never Never Land
where true love is entirely normal
and Yours Sincerely not just formal,
a country of the mind, Utopian,
where no one knows about Fallopian
tubes, or impotence; abortions
aren't individual fruit pie portions
served to so many. It's all jokey,
Lambeth Walk, and hokey-cokey,
schoolboy humour. Surely BUM FACE
must be the jolly mask for some face
that has known how what's distressing
isn't much relieved by dressing
up in whiskers and false noses?
DESPERATE DAN, as one supposes,
is much closer to what lovers
usually find; his one line covers
with its sad, trite declaration
lifetimes of the desperation
most must meet with the Romantic—
that both delights and drives us frantic.

DAISY FROM BUNNY

In a *Tales From Boccaccio* (1899), illustrated
by Byam Shaw in a William Morrissy style
and "done into English" by Joseph Jacobs
(in whose Introduction it is stated
that stories which now raise a smile
in smoking rooms—an oral tradition—
were then "published unblushingly" by men of erudition),

on the slightly foxed fly-leaf, drawn in Indian ink, clearly,
appears in the top left hand corner a single flower
linked by a Gothic "from" in the page's centre
to a bottom right hand corner rabbit. Merely
that and nothing more. The power
of the pictographs was thought sufficient;
amusing, intimate, and obviously not deficient—

in cosiness, coyness (our view) or (theirs?) emotion.
How very English, we feel. The rabbit is not badly drawn.
The four *Tales* are not the sexy ones. The problem
is this. We still can have no notion,
was he a cousin or, lovelorn,
after Daisy, Fleur, Marguerite? It's funny
how copulation and cuddliness are combined in a name
                                                    like Bunny.

"BRILLIANT SPY AND TOTALLY INADEQUATE MAN"
—The Spectator on a character of John Le Carré

Last seen in a bar called "The Whore's Shoe".
  Gone fishing with an agent out of Prague.
A life constructed of episodes.
Notes on the piano, ambiguous to the last.

Nothing rhymes. It's just a syllable
  count. It's Time that carries you on, from one
electric second of the clock's tick
to the next—and all it means is purely nothing.

Knitting is what it's like, long stories
  where stitches link in line like woolly spies—
networks and cover, safe houses, who's
blown? Your mind must hold it all in place, like knitting.

Boring it certainly is—and quite
  fairly futile. Messages from Control
sometimes come through but praise is rare and
letter-placing arduous; from within, boring.

Mole. Into that foreign soil burrowed,
  a fox among the Philistines—Nature
provides parallels, host/parasite;
so does History. Zeebrugge too had a mole.

Man you are and secret. If the cap
  fits, wear it. All you'll get from literates,
in human terms sad, this epitaph:
"brilliant spy and totally inadequate man".

SEPTEMBER CRICKET, 1975

The rough brown grass at the edge of the field
where the spectators are sitting
is dappled with dead leaves (the wind lifts
them misleadingly like butterflies, and sifts
through the dryness; summer was hard-hitting).
Quiet cricket, no drama—unless someone appealed—

but for one wasp, two flies, that grass is insect-dead.
It could be, easily, fifty
years ago—the same houses, the same church—
we can say, without benefit of research,
that time, spendthrift changer, was thrifty
and changed most of this only in the head.

The clothes of the watchers and the shapes of the cars
parked round the Common
are really the only specific outward signs
that we run our lives now on different lines
since they died at Mons, on the Somme, on
those battlefields now as remote as Mars—

and we've had our own wars, big and small.
No change in the middle
with bowlers, batsmen, overs and pads—
but apart from the players (the local lads),
a few wives and kids (this is the riddle),
almost nobody is watching this game at all!

Apart from myself, just three separate old men—
count them on the fingers
of some televisual technological hand.

29

Yet this is Village Cricket, you understand,
an Old English thing, that still lingers
and keeps going unfailingly, like Big Ben—

so they all wishfully hope and say.
Don't let's be elegiac,
too many people are. Even with folk lore,
it's always far better to know the score
(give up head-hunting, like the head-hunting Dyak).
Perhaps, in a sunny September, village cricket has had its day?

THE PRICE OF THINGS

"What aspect does the unwisdom take?"
"Certain absorbition. I have other and terribly important things
to do. The husband is most worthy, one wonders what the next
few years will bring. Their temperaments must be as the poles."
—Elinor Glyn, *The Price of Things*.

The moralists say there's a price
for the pleasures that make the brain swoony,
    and all those who have them must pay;

so the fiery tempestuous mates
in love stories by passionate women
    have their troubles—although they succeed

in the end with a baby and bliss
(in this kind of fantasy usual).
    And the "all for love", as they say,

works out well for the family name
but the scented half-Turkish pretender
    is exposed as the man that he is,

as a taker of drugs and the slave
of the beautiful sensual spy; she
    has her firing squad at Vincennes.

While grey-eyed Amaryllis Ardayre
sees the war take her impotent husband
    (a hunting accident here

has made him entirely no good—
says a surgeon of fame, Lemon Bridges)
    and can marry his cousin. She sees

"how extraordinarily well his bronze hair
was planted" (it reads) "on his forehead . . . "
    By a trick, he has slept with her, to

    ensure that there will be an heir—
she didn't know it was him, it was all the result of collusion.
    There has always been an Ardayre

    at Ardayre. What the average girl
thought of this, in the Twenties, I wonder
    as I read through each brown-white foxed page.

    Did they know it was all make-believe?
And what about poor Edith Thompson—
    perhaps for her it was real,

    and she felt it her Duty to Love
as she read all those novels of High Life
    where the heroines fascinate men

    in the Carlton, Brook Street, or the Ritz?
Scents, jewels, cigarettes, pianos, brandy—
    to set off *her* beauty, of course—

    and the tête-à-tête dinners with wine!
When she ended up labelled a Temptress
    that all decent women would shun,

    unpredictably cast as The Spy
and hauled to that drugged execution,
    did she think it was cheap at the price?

32

If you see reality clear
with its blackheaded face in the mirror,
   this may be a far better thing

   than the daydream that goes with champagne
and wakes up with a hangover, blinking,
   to the terrible trap in the floor.

A PASSIONATE WOMAN

As I stood there in my tea-gown,
   picture of a passionate woman,
I shot him six times, brain matter
fresh from the head wounds.

And the first shot was for the vulva,
   the hot revenge of a lover,
I had the gun now, lead semen
splurged in his soft flesh.

The clitoris triggered second:
   hating his questing mouth-tongue,
it hit him, swelled with blood-anger,
surfeit and tasting.

The third one was for the anus,
   fingered and pricked so often,
an exit used as an entry,
tender, resentful.

The fourth bullet had nipples
   written all over it—
they were so bitten, erected,
stood up like cobras.

The fifth came straight from the labia,
   frivolously toyed with,
brushed aside mostly; neglectful,
his mouth paid blood money.

The sixth avenged my own mouth,
   forced to the licking cocksuck
by my own desires; mouthfuls
it gave him—not of kisses.

TO THE DEAD

You were there with a glass in your hand,
   and loving it so—
I confess that I don't understand
   why you had to go.

You were smoking your head off and gay—
   now you're not there.
Was it something I said? didn't say?
   It isn't fair.

You were rogering several girls,
   enjoying it a lot—
a privileged swine among pearls—
   and now you're not.

You had all the best cards in the deck
   a moment ago—
then you sank out of sight like a wreck,
   why, I don't know.

You vanished so quickly it's hard
   to account for your choice.
Did a doom turn up with a card—
   or a Master's voice?

THE GODS OF THE COPYBOOK HEADINGS

In May 1976, forty years after Kipling's death, a class of thirteen adult British "O" Level English Language students had never heard of Kipling, nor had they heard of any of his books (even the children's books), though one student thought he might have written poems. Another asked if he was anything to do with Mr. Kipling's Cakes.—*Author's Note*.

Though you use Old Testament phrases, as Biblical as could be,
When you're pushing up the daisies you will certainly agree
That even the Best get forgotten (we're an absent-minded lot),
The Good Tree with the Rotten, if they're not there on the spot.

You can write like a Cockney soldier an' show yer bleedin'
                                                        'eart—
When your bones are growing mouldier than they ever were at
                                                    the start
They'll be asking "Who was Atkins?" with a blank and
                                            mystified stare,
There'll be daffodils and catkins, in a Spring when you're not
                                                        there.

You can write the Great Short Stories, on the sentimental side,
With the politics pleasing to Tories, and lament how the loved
                                                    ones died.
You can fill them with genuine feeling (and dialect), all your
                                                        skill
Won't make them much more appealing to Time, as he moves
                                                    on still.

Remember it has been written how *Those to whom Evil is done
Do Evil*; and, Once Bitten, when your life had scarcely begun,

37

You might develop a Trauma and turn into a Bully yourself—
Not the Latter or the Former will stay long on the library shelf.

The Gods of the Copybook Headings treat even Good Writers
with scorn,
They don't reckon much with our weddings and how many
children were born.
They are Anglo-Saxon and clannish; like their Copybooks,
dated too.
They, too, in the end will vanish—and so, I'm afraid, will you.

WHAT IT IS

It's very like a sneeze
that can, partly, be controlled by the will—
it's postponed only, it's sure to come,
and a lot of the pleasure is in the postponement,
the delayed explosion.

It's like sawing wood;
two people with a two-handed saw
pull in an ecstasy of rhythm,
increasing the speed with each stroke
until they are through.

It's like a little death,
a falling through consciousness into oblivion,
a peculiar kind of peace, after
the unarmed combat, the struggle—
deep rest after effort.

E. Jarvis-Thribb (17) and Keith's Mum
don't reckon you;
even students of English get lost
in your syntax,
the long sentences and the Greek idioms
("he knew to build")
confuse the lovers of what's simple,
the multitudinous
classical allusions just fill them with boredom.
Eliot's hypothesis
was that your magniloquence led on to Wordsworth
and Coleridge, poets
who could write (or talk) the hind leg off a donkey.

You didn't have much use for humour,
wit vanished early
from your verse (in any sense) and rhyme
you thought barbarous;
perhaps in your day nothing much was funny,
as now in Ulster,
and how could you have the needed detachment?
But like a rocket
you took off for outer space and the SF demons,
you really did go
into overdrive, no short-haul aircraft,
medium range bomber
or helicopter, but a giant blockbuster.

So for this kind of verse, which has a genuine grandeur,
you are the best one—
Wordsworth's dim mountains are only molehills,
I think, compared.

You truly invented your own mighty language—
like Ulysses' bow,
nobody else could handle it; *it* bent *them*.
Of course you took sides
and suffered for it; if pride was your fault, still
you had cause for that.
The young undergraduate of Christ's College
combing his long blond hair
with an ivory comb? As well as arrogance, beauty.

THE LADY LEFT BEHIND

"When boys and girls go out to play there is always someone
left behind, and the boy who is left behind is no use to the girl
who is left behind."—Paul Potts, *Dante Called You Beatrice*.

The affaires of the Spring and Summer are already under way
but nobody looks at *me* yet, as day succeeds to day,
and nobody *will* look at me—this is my constant fear—
through all the days of sunshine and all the coming year.

Each morning I look in the mirror, I see an older face,
the face of someone defeated—without charm, without grace.
I see the couples together, sitting and drinking wine.
They look into each other's eyes—no one looks into mine.

They're saying "But you're beautiful!" and pressing hands
(or feet)
secretly in the restaurant. No one says "You're so sweet!"
or sits at *my* lonely table. I feel the waiters sneer—
permanently on the waiting list, without a cavalier.

Everyone thinks it's funny. I'm spoiling for a man,
"on the shelf", a "spinster", a "frustrated" also-ran.
So many jokes on the telly! Jokes that everyone's heard—
but a human being *can* spoil, you know; spoiling's the right
word!

HOW TRAGEDY IS IMPOSSIBLE

There are sorrows in herds that are too deep for words,
                    and the true concentration camp horror
isn't lessened by sighs; if, by torture, one dies it isn't much
                    use saying "Begorrah!"
and it's perfectly clear that to murmur "Oh, dear!" as you
                    fall from the face of the Eiger
or to mouth "Me, oh my!" (an inadequate cry) when you're
                    bitten in half by a tiger
can by no means express your true state of distress. Will
                    Shakespeare was once reckoned clever
but the nearest he got to that sensitive spot was "Never,
                    never, never, never, never!"

For the words are too weak. To moan "Oimoi!" in Greek
                    was no better than our interjections.
It is simply a sound we can get our tongues round with a
                    varying force and inflexions
but it doesn't explain or make clear, or complain, with
                    anything much that's specific,
and the brain is quite numb (that is what makes us dumb) in
                    the face of the really horrific.
What you feel is immense, but beyond sound and sense; and
                    the shock is a strong anaesthetic,
for what knocks you right out can't be said in a shout. And
                    all such attempts are pathetic.

It's the same with our love (rhymes are 'dove' and 'above',
                    and nothing much else that's romantic);
you adore her big eyes (and her hand on your flies) and this
                    passion is making you frantic,
and you dote to excess—but until you undress there is no
                    cogent way to convey it.

It's a very odd thing, that (perhaps) you can sing and (just)
                    feel, think or touch—but not *say* it.
For our loves are like surds and too way out for words; finite
                    terms of our ordinary numbers
can't express them at all, they drive us up the wall—and
                    archaic, with 'smitten' and 'slumbers'.

But there's one kind of Muse who will never refuse, except
                    when the bombs are atomic,
to provide a good phrase, who is always in phase with events
                    —and you could call her Comic,
though her humour's quite wry, rational, even dry on
                    occasion. And yet her wild farces
succeed time and again—while the serious men, striking
                    attitudes, end on their arses—
because, you will find, they appeal to the mind and they've
                    not blown their top with emotion
and it's better to think than to take drugs or drink— you
                    might even avoid that explosion!

Section 2

OH, DARLING!

"Oh, darling, I've brought you a present,
    it's here by the side of the bed,
by your beautiful plump naked bottom
    and your beautiful feminine head.
Move over and let me show you,
    reclined like an odalisque there
with your breasts like two soft circles
    and triangular pubic hair."

"Oh, darling, it looks Victorian!
    Such a box! of such lovely wood!
Is it mother of pearl at the corners?
    You have always understood
how a woman adores *surprises*!
    and the nice unexpected things
(like red roses, a film, or a theatre)
    are exciting as diamond rings!"

"Oh, darling, I wanted to please you,
    I went to a very good shop
to buy something to keep us together
    and ensure that our loves never stop.
It's a gift of the gods—you could call it
    a bond that binds more than a kiss—
among all of the other antiques there
    there was nothing as fine as this!"

"Oh, darling! But how does it open?
    It looks so polished and clean—
but is there a key to go with it,
    or do you press something? I mean,

47

I can't see a sign of a keyhole.
    Oh, it *slides*! How ingenious, dear!
Let me move a bit, so I can kiss you—
    but *please* don't bite my ear!"

"Oh, darling, you've taken the lid off,
    so tell me at once what you see—
for you it may not have the meaning
    that it has, never doubt it, for me!
It is more than a beautiful symbol,
    it's a practical means to an end,
it's a lover whose love is eternal
    and a permanent faithful friend!"

"Oh, darling, you've loved me and kissed me,
    you've shown me a barrel of fun,
and a thousand good times with your ardour,
    so why—now—do you show me a *gun*?
I can see it's an old-fashioned pistol,
    it's lovely, but has it been fired?
With such things, I must tell you, my darling,
    I'm really a terrible coward!"

"Oh, darling, I asked. It's a virgin,
    as it lies there with its deathly gleam,
and nobody yet has exploited
    its potential, fulfilling the dream!
As it lies there, on pale lilac velvet,
    so snugly indented, so cold,
don't you see it is Love, even Youth, there—
    and a charm against us growing old!"

"Oh, darling! But why do you glare so?
  Is it *loaded*? I guess by your eyes!
They are savaging me, sad and lionlike!
  This is quite an *unpleasant* surprise!
I was glad (it's aimed at me! Oh, Heaven!)
  to assist in the sexual act
(Please, please, darling, don't pull the trigger!)
  but *not* in a Suicide pact!"

We could be chums, you and I,
   And in greatness of heart we could dare—
As the sun is steadfast in the sky
   We two could be constant there;
For a man and a woman in love
   Reckon not of the changing of Time
As the hand fits so close in the glove
   And heartbeats rhyme!

I could match with an ardent soul
   Your longings to hold me close
While the bells of the earthbound toll
   In the lives of the dull and gross!
Yea, we could ascend on high
   Above the unfeeling old earth!
Oh, will you not echo the cry
   And give it birth?

Shall the twain never be as one
   As we float far and free as a bird
In the smile of the beaming sun,
   Borne aloft o'er the teeming herd?
Oh, tell me now, dear, of those wings
   That could lift us both, carrying you
To my land where pure happiness sings
   Up in the blue!

To that peak where the mist-cloud is curled
   Let us strive, in a union so blest
That it takes no account of the World
   Where the mercen'ry gain is the best—

Let us love, in our loving so brave
    That in loving alone is our pride,
True chums, that is all that I crave,
    And side by side!

PERCHANCE A JEALOUS FOE

It was Spring when Annabel came to Stoatswold.
The old house lay slumbering in the warm Spring sunshine
as though waiting for something to happen. Nothing happened.
The smoke just curled up lazily from Elizabethan chimneys
as it had for generations of incumbent Stoatswolds,
an old family and proud of it—from before the Normans.
(In fact, the present owner was Sir Norman Stoatswold,
a widower who smoked a pipe in the Long Garden
and was well-known locally for the quality of his shorthorns).

Annabel came, of course, as a governess. Her young charge
was pretty little Myfanwy Stoatswold, fifteen and headstrong.
She was called Myfanwy because her dead mother
had been a Welsh Nationalist (and hated Suffolk).
Annabel often wondered if she would have been called Fiona
if the nationality had been otherwise. She never asked him.
Sir Norman was a man's man, and only spoke in monosyllables.
He was very gruff and shy and terrified of women,
much preferring his pipe. Annabel gave him
his favourite tobacco for his forty-fifth birthday.
His eyes seemed to light up with a brief understanding.

Myfanwy was a bit of a minx but everyone loved her.
A madcap girl who rode tractors side-saddle
and was on good terms with all the farmhands,
she nevertheless used to split the infinitive
and her spelling was atrocious. Annabel often
wondered if she would ever pass her "O" Level English—
though she thought she might do well as a liberated woman,
with all that money. Annabel herself came
from the large family of an impoverished clergyman.
She was cheerful but indigent.

Time went by, and one day succeeded another.
At a party in the nearby market town,
to which Annabel had been invited by accident,
she met Sebastian Anchovy, a sophisticated novelist
and a member of another old County family—
carried away by an impulse and without really meaning to,
she took his side in an argument with Emery Sandpiper,
the Cockney critic, very brash and abrasive from his TV
                                                  appearances,
who was saying how Margaret Drabble was really thick.
Annabel bristled with offended sensibility
and Sebastian said calmly: "I beg to differ".
Later he slipped her a joint in the bathroom
and they achieved a certain *rapport* of fellow feeling,
as he explained to her how Oxford wasn't Cambridge.

After that they continued to meet fairly often.
For afternoons together they would go off cycling,
wobbling through the primroses. Once Sebastian
laid a hand on her knee as they sat in a tea room.
Annabel knew he was beginning to care for her.
He even came to Stoatswold, and talked about shorthorns.
They would all three be sitting, with glasses of cowslip wine
(Myfanwy, the tomboy, was out shooting rabbits
in the company of a ferret called Fred),
and Sebastian would discourse at length about his ancestors.
Sir Norman said nothing, but carefully refilled his pipe.
In these conversations he was a kind of smoke-screen,
under cover of which Sebastian made advances.

Finally Annabel allowed him to kiss her.
They became engaged—but were keeping it secret
because of his mother, old Lady Anchovy.
Sir Norman was silent but seemed rather moody—

you could never tell what he was thinking.
Myfanwy had a crush on a cowhand called Joe
and was oblivious to everything that happened around her.

Nothing did happen—which was standard and
par for the course, as Sebastian might have said
in his civilised manner. Until one evening,
when Sir Norman had certainly taken
far more cowslip wine than was really good for him,
he dropped a pipe and broke it. "Oh, flip!" he shouted.
Annabel was amazed to hear him swearing—
he was the sort of man who says "Ladies present!"—
so she stared at him. "What are you staring at,
you sly little puss?!" Sir Norman bellowed.
"I've seen you with Sebastian in the rhododendrons!"

Annabel caught a hanky to her eyes and rushed from the room.
At breakfast the next morning, over his scrambled eggs,—
Sir Norman apologised. Later that day
he brushed against her, accidentally, in a passage.
Annabel felt the blood rising to her face. Abruptly
he seized her. "Oh, Annabel! My darling!
How can I live without you?" Impulsively
he strained her to him. His moustache on her forehead
tickled her slightly—but quickly she realised
how her feeling for Sebastian was terribly superficial.
"Let me think!" she riposted; and half an hour later
the engagement was broken; and in the late summer
she became Lady Stoatswold. And in her honour
Myfanwy changed the name of her favourite ferret
and called her Annabel—she was the wife of Fred.

THE THIRTIES LOVE LYRIC

I follow you in my mind,
I see you each day,
how you go on your way,
and I watch you so fai-
thfully then,
as you walk about among men!

If they should pinch your behind
or stroke a big boob
in the closely-packed Tube
that would just be the Rub-
icon, when
you walk so aloof among men!

I'm with you now in the spirit, close,
so near you—though we're parted—
and I don't need to be too verbose
to say I'm broken-hearted . . .

My thoughts follow you as you find
your sweet way to the office and all of those coff-
ees, they stick close as toff-
ees, dear, when
you go out to work among men!

I still watch over you, kind,
(though it seems very trite)
when you come home at night—
avoid boys who get tight,
darling, then
you might live so safe among men!

You are the fruit, I'm the rind,
and I'm there to protect
though the worst I expect
is you won't be select-
ive, quite, when
you're offered the friendship of men!

I'm never far, though I'm miles away,
I see you very clearly,
I'm counting hours till that distant day
when I'm more than Yours sincerely . . .

These are the links that can bind—
though the boss is your type,
with blue eyes and a pipe,
please ignore all his hyp-
erbole—then
you'll still be mine among men!

THE REVIEWING OF POETRY

So your new book's just out? You should splash wine about—
                      for this must be a joyful occasion?
Not at all! you reply to that questioning eye, for the critical
                      gift of "abrasion"
is the one that's most favoured—you're salt that's not
                      savoured; reviewers must be *entertaining*
(readers must have their fun)—though they're in a bright sun,
                      they will tell their dim public it's raining
if this makes a good story, for a journalist's glory is to stir
                      up those somnolent morons
who have much less idea of the art we have here than a tribe
                      of illiterate Hurons!
Circulation's shoe pinches—they waste column inches on
                      mocking the innocent photos
of the authors on jackets (like flowers on seed packets)—then
                      proceed with andante con motos
to lament with a tear how it doesn't appear, although *their*
                      attempts are so gallant
that a person could find, unless out of his mind, the slightest
                      small vestige of talent
in this tedious verbiage that runs wild like herbage all over
                      the pitiful pages.
But if Truth's what you want, from an unsullied font, you
                      should know that it isn't for ages
or possibly ever that he's been so clever (athough he's
                      devoted to Culture)
to sort out in his head what's worthwhile that he's read or to
                      tell a good verse from a vulture!
It's so safe, though, mock-sad, to call everything bad; no one
                      then can say you were a sucker
if the fashion should change and you had to arrange to revive
                      that young lad Tommy Tucker

as inspired "Nursery Folk"—and this isn't a joke— it could
                              happen and maybe to-morrow
(and with no thought of merit—a rabbit's a ferret for *them*
                              and a Cotman a Corot)
that for Gunn and Ted Hughes we read "Rhythm and Blues"
                    in half-with-it, half-in school anthologies
where a bad word like "bed", if it raises its head, is quite
                              stifled at once with apologies—
for as everyone knows from his head to his toes (or her toes)
                              there is no animality
in a teenager's heart. They are pure in each part, and the
                    word they've not heard's "sexuality"!
What they don't understand, critics blast out of hand—they're
                    spectators who don't know the rules well
in a whole lot of cases, but they don't hide their faces! They
                    will say that they don't suffer fools well
and with no hint of shame they will go on to blame the poor
                              writer; it's very much harder
to produce wholesome food than to write something rude
                    pointing out that there's zilch in the larder!
For it's hard to create. And it's Art that they hate. It's not
                    newsworthy—nobody cares much,
readers don't want to know; it seems baiting a poet's just
                    fun—as it once was with bears, much
less exciting perhaps, more like throwing of craps—but it
                    raises *your* temperature highly,
paranoia is throbbing, there's sighing and sobbing, and those
                    darts have gone home, oh, so slyly—

for you can't bear to look at your miserable book, and a
needless bad line drills a hole in your spine, and you feel
you would like someone's head on a spike and—of true
SF size, just to kick in their eyes—centipedes in big boots,
to reduce their gay hoots to a terrible scream, make their

58

life a bad dream, as you burn for revenge from **Pitlochry to Penge**, and you feel all your efforts are wasted;

but at least the book's out (to a jeer or a shout) and, although you feel vexed, you can start on the next— and it couldn't be *more* panned and pasted!

A WEE SANG FOR ST. ANDREW'S DAY

Wha dreams that I am nae a Scot,
Yon is a blastit Hottentot,
A rude uneducatit clot—
   In Southron speech—
Lang may his cods unusit rot,
   Craibs bite his breech!

May nae wlonk wink him wi' her ee,
May mini-sarks his presence flee
An' houghmagandie sic as he
   Ay strang avoid;
His lume til that he comes to dee
   A' unemployed!

I canna thole sic wallidrags—
Auld Scots an' new my Musie brags,
She can blaw baith on tartan bags
   Wi' canty mou';
The Saltire's on the best 'o flags
   When I am fou!

What though I live by London's wa'?
I ken richt weil the waups that ca'
The hairts o' Scots, aye, ane an' a',
   Baith rich an' puir;
I ken too Celtic an' fitba',
   The burn an' muir.

Sae let nae daft presumptuous loon
Wha's plaid's a stiflin' word-cocoon
Preach Lallans tae me, late an' soon.

There's mony a sang
In mony a tongue aneath the moon—
And nane is wrang!

cods	*balls*	wallidrags	*weaklings*
craibs	*crabs*	bags	*bagpipes*
wlonk	*lovely lady*	canty	*happy*
mini-sarks	*shortie nighties* (cf. "cutty sark")	mou	*mouth*
		fou	*drunk*
houghmagandie	*fornication*	waups	*curlews*
lume	*penis*		
		fitba'	*football*
thole	*endure*		

Lallans   *Lowland Scots*

THE NOBLE ENGLISH TRAVELLER
CONTEMPLATES TURKISH DELIGHT

That heavy-featured Turkish face
reminds me of another place;
for most of 1873
we shall be joined in buggeree.

Your harem trousers filled with grace
are like balloons in Chevy Chase;
you are the most delightful she
I ever filled with buggeree.

You flap and flop like dab or dace
as I increase my headlong pace;
I feel you doubled under me.
in quintessential buggeree.

And as I ride and as I race
no gentleman jockey trumps my ace;
as sweating under the Turkish tree
you suffer the joys of buggeree.

So far from Western fur and lace,
fat nakedness is no disgrace;
you only feel completely free
in the male grip of buggeree.

"A GOOD MOUSE NEEDS NO PREPARATION"

—Interview with a policeman, breeder of prize-winning mice,
broadcast 9th June 1975 on BBC 4.

This is an age
when people throw Life quivering on the page,
    untidy, crude;
or on a screen or canvas—hot and nude
    the Muse lies there
gasping, quite unadorned, completely bare,
    while all agree
if she were clothed she wouldn't then be She.
    Her lovers, firm
in adoration, pour out words like sperm.
    The act is all—
simple intensity, the mating call
    we recognise.
Bras, panties, hats are inessential lies.

A certain truth
such wooers have, though they are so uncouth.
    Some passionate thought
must still be there; the skilful and untaught
    alike must bring
a kind of ardour—or the words won't sing.
    The pulsing heart
romantically throbs in the best Art,
    but not direct;
for we should emphasize, refine, select.
    Pejorative word,
it's "artificial", but it's not absurd,
    wrong, or ungood,
to carve the statue from the native wood.

Tool-making man
always improves on Nature, if he can.
    The critic raves
about those buffaloes painted in caves
    so long ago.
This is what's called "technique" (you want to know?),
    magic or not;
it's what we have and animals haven't got.
    Some wash their mice
(painting is not allowed) to make them nice,
    or use a comb.
I'm on their side—a house is not a home,
    and caring helps
verse, painting, music, mice, cubs, kittens, whelps.

LEAVING LEEDS*

* "I used once to be plagued with a man who wrote verses, but who literally had no other notion of a verse, but that it consisted of ten syllables. *Lay your knife and your fork across your plate*, was to him a verse:

"Lay your knife and your fork, across your plate."
—Boswell's *Life of Johnson*,
quoted by Roy Fuller in *Owls and Artificers*

Lay your knife and your fork, across your plate,
see the sun as it shines, on yellow egg,
brighter certainly too, your bacon gone.
Coffee! Coffee! Four cups, awakened now,
(Yorkshire breakfast, ee lad, a champion meal)
smoke, enjoy the cigar, a footbridge waits,
cross it, handle your bag, a London train!

In, then, quick! To relax, ignore the child
climbing over your knee, complacent mum,
dad with sport and the nudes, the daily dose,
football godlike and good, the city's love.
Hear the voice of a girl, a children's nurse
come from Cromer to York, returning now,
saying "Difficult! Yes, a father's boy!"

Yesterday you were there, to read some verse,
students' listening beards, refused the mike,
spoke it cosily too, elitist crap
they thought, probably; rhyme, who really now
needs it? formalist yet, bad marks from Marx!
Golden oldies are few, ambitions make
swollen heads and bad thoughts, not very nice.

Softly dieseling through, the train is calm,
lunch comes charmingly round, a soothing time,

hearing opposite men, the business ones,
talking, knowing, of cars, the horsepower boys.
Life is various too, and we have luck—
starving, beaten, diseased, no, that we're not.
Countries prosper or fail, get down and out.

Systems need to be changed, and that's the truth.
Money, profit and work, they wear us down,
sacred cows of our life, that don't regard
verse's stresses and strains, yet these at least,
harmless, innocent, clear, are playful ploys
exercised for us all, to entertain.
Boswell's comma is fun, but not for us.

THE IMMENSE ADVANTAGE

"I was thinking you might like gooseberry tart and cream for a sweet, miss."
Oh that I could have vented my New World enthusiasm in a shriek of delight as I heard those intoxicating words, heretofore met only in English novels!"—Kate Douglas Wiggin, *A Cathedral Courtship* (1893).

"A hundred years ago, England had over America what Emerson called 'the immense advantage'. American thoughts, he wrote, were English thoughts. Today it would be as true to say that America has the advantage over Europe."—Stephen Spender. 1973.

Aw, shit, man!
What's England compared to Whitman?
Or being British
(though DHL was so cuntish and tittish)?
Even Creeley
is as way-out to *them* as stoned Swahili,
great bearded Ginsberg
is a frightening outer suburb of old-time Sinsburg.
All effete cultures
wind up, as they should, in the claws of the vultures.

I intention
to nominate the whole gang as a lavender convention,
once-English Auden
a has-been golden oldie as square as Trollope's Warden.
"Be a Star-screwer!"
yelled Corso, fuck-holes mesmerised McClure—
that's good yelling!
& fuck the Past and all punctuation and spelling!

yeah, rhyme is
far better left to those effeminate limeys.

Old Blakey
was a throbbing poet-guru and no mistakey,
like me—bearded—
and he saw the cockeyed world like no other seer did.
They don't dig, son,
though there are traces of Early American in old Geoff
                                                    Grigson,
a few imitators
have raised the Stars and Stripes among those masturbators—
but don't bet on it,
most of those creeps are still writing the fucking Sonnet!

As a scene it's crappy—
no wonder those faggy Britlits are so unhappy.
The parameters
only allow them to get high on iambic pentameters—
if A-M-E-R-I-C-A
went down on them with a passio hysterica
they'd be so excited
their cocksucking pin-striped pants would get ignited!
They'd be creaming
with continuous wall-to-wall high-pitched screaming!

Don't dig Dallas,
don't dig Zukovsky's inprovements to Catullus,
don't dig Berryman,
get hooked on the novels of H. Seton Merriman—
believe me, buddy,
if they tried (and they do try) they couldn't be more
                                                    fuddy-duddy.

It's overshoes and mufflers
for that bunch of arthritic motherfucking snufflers.
AMERICA, be up and doing!
let's take a goddam trip, let's get Star-screwing!

PASTORAL

Dominic Francis Xavier Brotherton-Chancery
had an egg for breakfast every morning
and revelled in obsolete forms. For example
he called an eclogue an eglog (like the Elizabethans).
He went everywhere on a bicycle. He knew very well
that ordinary people had never heard of an eclogue.
How he despised them! When his rough friend
made savage fun of Gerard Manley Hopkins,
jokingly speaking of "The Burglar's First Communion"
and hinting at the lust concealed in a work called

"Hairy Ploughman",

although he giggled Dominic was shocked—
such a lack of Faith! But what he loved in his friend
was exactly the shaggy goat-footed Philistine roughness,
it made *him* seem at least twice as cultivated.
His coarse moustache was an animal temptation.
His coltish clumsiness—oh, Dominic adored!
They were both sheepheards. His mother was a nymphe.
The sheepheardesses lived in a different valley.
He literally wanted (as Gus guffawed)
no part of them! Lithe on his bicycle
he rode contented through a summer idyll.

THE TREE OF KNOWLEDGE

"They tell you about love and romance, and then the first thing
you see is this huge purple thing."—Disillusioned girl, quoted
in an article on Rape by Katharine Whitehorn, *The Observer*,
1st June, 1975.

That dubious *They*
means teachers—not seducers in the hay,
    presumably,
sweet-talkers with one hand above the knee.
    Those magazines
that tell of love and husbands, with such scenes
    censored right out—
they cause some trouble, there can be no doubt.
    Romantic songs
feature a world all right, without such wrongs;
    and everything
that tells girls happiness lies in a ring,
    religions, too,
prepare with ignorance of what is blue,
    rustic and worse,
and bring their own particular kind of curse.

Hear Virtue's yelp!
But crying "Wicked!" doesn't really help.
    The growing boys
see girls as objects, not much more than toys;
    experiment
belongs to youth, as hops belong to Kent.
    And circumstance
alters each case, a man who takes his chance
    need not be bad;
an untouched girl can end up very sad.

While Nature too
has put a Life Force into me and you
        that has no use
for morals either (this is no excuse,
        but does explain)—
though one quick pleasure causes so much pain.

        Mind-readers grow
after a time instinctively to know,
        one must suppose,
which girls, and when, want to take off their clothes;
        being roughly wooed
some find enjoyable as well as crude.
        What is offence
to one could be another's commonsense—
        don't get me wrong,
I'm certainly not bursting into song
        in praise of rape,
so brutal in its every form or shape.
        I sympathise
with that sour girl; the sight that met her eyes
        could cause alarm
to unbriefed virgins—but for some has charm.

        Illusions can't
keep out experience, a maiden aunt
        Life never was.
But nor can Reason, with its wise "because",
        soften the blow
entirely; yet it's surely best to know
        what to expect?
Erectile tissue loves to stand erect
        (in women too),
it shouldn't come at you out of the blue.

Someone should *tell*,
before the scuffling and that outraged yell;
an educated guess
as to which man thinks No's a disguised Yes
can't come amiss.

To save us all from articles like this.

HEREWARD THE WEAK

Hereward Holyoak was a not inconsiderable twithound,
he lived in Marsh Road, not so far from the Gas Works,
and was (as it were mentally) monarch of all he surveyed.
He never went for exciting rides on the bodies of girls,
though he made a few journeys on the naughty 69 bus.
The office he worked in seemed to be run by the Romans
(not even the Danes); of Gadwine and Stigand,
Bishop Aegelwine and Saint Sexburga he knew nothing.
He was neither a berserker, a brain-hewer, nor a sea-thief
and the only Norman he knew was called Norman Pringle.
He had no wife called Torfrida, brought back from Flanders,
and certainly not a second wife called Aelfryth.
If Doreen Upminster looked at him, he blushed.
The tea-ladies thought he was a nice boy but backward.
He was never a victim of the blandishments of Alftruda,
none of his enemies were cloven to the chine—
though he once gave Mr. Robinson a dirty look.
He never, ever, ate cormorant pie.

Is it better to be like this, I wonder,
than to bugger up the life-style of the Isle of Ely?

"IT'S HARD TO DISLIKE EWART"
—New Review critic

I always try to dislike my poets,
it's good for them, they get so uppity otherwise,
going around thinking they're little geniuses—
but sometimes I find it hard. They're so pathetic
in their efforts to be *liked*.
When we're all out walking on the cliffs
it's always pulling my coat with "Sir! Oh, Sir!"
and "May I walk with *you*, Sir?"—
I sort them out harshly with my stick.

If I push a few over the edge, that only
encourages the others. In the places of preferment
there is room for just so many.
The rest must simply lump it.
There's too much sucking up and trying to be clever.
They must all learn they'll never get round *me*.
Merit has nothing to do with it. There's no way
to pull the wool over my eyes, *no* way,
no way . . .

Section 3

VARIATIONS AND EXCERPTS
("Ballocky Bill The Sailor")

Who's that crepitating with his knuckledusters on my portico?
Who's the man aggressifying his digits on my doorbox?
Who is the person terrifying the nightwood with his fistfuls?
    cried the beauteous young virgin
       (called the youthful female winner of Beauty Prizes)
       (enunciated the scarcely mature attractive lady)

It is only I from the mighty recesses of Ocean, cried William,
the Mightily-testiculated Mariner
(At your service, my Lady, from the scaly squadrons' lair,
intimated Guglielmo, the Man of Parts, the Seafarer)
(Here I am after a rough crossing, said Willie the Well-
endowed Water-wanderer)

I will descend then and admit you
I'll go below and allow you up
'Tis I will sink that you may rise
    cried the freshly formed teenage trollop
       (lisped her lovely under-twenty Ladyship)
       (opined the new slick chick)

I am ancient and rugose and a stranger to the bath and yet
vigorous, yelled Will the Well-hung Matelot
(Many summers have I seen, my skin is no longer smooth,
nor is it sanitate, but I maintain my strength, cracked Billy
the Ballsy Bo'sun)
(No more am I youthful, my manners are crude, I am not
well-washed, but I am nevertheless full of energy, explained
Guillaume the Big-balled Waterman) . . .

FOUR VARIATIONS

Esmeraldo could hear Cloalda singing, down in the patio.
"A girl like de cocktalk!
A girl like de suckfuck!"

It was an old tune from the Twenties ("Then I'll be happy"),
and it carried with it emotional "overtones".

Green could hear Chlo humming, alone in the yard:
"Mm mm mm mm mm mm!
Mm mm mm mm mm mm!"

He recognised it as part of a new album by the Frigs
("Squaw Talk"). He really dug it—like crazy.

Esmintruderaldo identified the voice of Clotiobalda,
carrolling in the Palace garden.
"Non mi dice
di quel contorno!"

He knew it to be a Cavatina of great power, from the Second
Act of Panolio's "I Cicisbei di Londra". His emotions were
stirred.

Sir Esmo hearkened well—the pure tones of Cholestera
floated up to him from the waters of the moat.
"My heart is a-homing
To-yon where my love lies!"

'Twas an old air and brought with it the sadness and the
turbulence of days long gone.

Hairs is the head upon which all 'the Inds of the Wold' are come, and the eye-lads are a big worry. It is a booty brought out from within upon the flash, the deposit (it'll sell and sell) of deranged thoughts and elastic braveries and exquisite fashions. Set it for a muniment beside one of those white Greek bodices or beautiful trimmings of antiquity, and how would they be trebled by this booty, into which the mole with all its maladies has passed? All the torts and interferences of the wold have itched and modelled there, in that they have powder, to refine and make impressive the outward *femme*, the enemalism of Greece, lust of Roehm, the ravery of the middle urge with its spiritual ambition and impaginated loves, the return of the Pogo world, the sins of the Bourgeois. She is older than the docks among whom she sits; like the Empire, she has been dead many times, and learned the secrets of the grove; and has been a thriver of steep bees, and keeps their appalling ways about her; and practised on strange beds with Eastern searchers: and, as Elfrida, was the mother of Ellen of Hoy, and, as Faint Anne, the mother of Hairy; and all this has been to her but as the ground of flowers and fruits, and lives only in the jelly baby with which it has folded the ranging tenements, and singed the eyelids and the hands. The fanny of the perpetual wife, keeping together men's thousand experiences, is an old one; and madder thought has conceived the idea of womanity as caught open by (and coming, flup!) by herself, all codes of fault and strife. Shirtily Lady Leisure might stand as the embonpoint of the old fanny, the sin-hole of the maiden idea.

PROS

Many an actor is funtastically handiclapped by the
superphysical triviality of his profession. Even in their
daily confusation ectors and ectresses, with their obligatory
and supererogatory Southern English eccents, appear very
shellow. With their ecstatic stratospheric cries of "Dorling!"
they fill the air, apparent to one and all as the glick
inheritors of a Monty Banks tradition. Not one but is a
cater-cousin to Dr. Dulcamara, Doll Tearsheet and all old
and young pretenders. Ectoplasmic abreactions disturb the
West End atmosphere, there is severe penurious displacement
of provincial respiratory companies, unexplicated compound
fractures of early promise rapidly supervene, hero or heroine
are the drugs of choice, and the flight from reality is on!

Almost all writers, conversely, live virgin to the pubic
public, their intercourse limited to the printed pallid page.
It is not theirs but a voice vicarious that speaks the living
line; they inhabit inhibited ecstasies, molecular moles in
their eccentric electricity. Simple but sincere, since here and
there they cannot even (odd though it may seem) articulate,
they are dumb before their sharers, wistfully waiting for
the randy reader who could pick them up and enjoy them.
Some far-flung wharfinger, some tough sailor in a rough
jersey—Lili Marlen is their professional prototype. *Stop me
and buy one* their mutilated motto, as they salaciously solicit,
standing beneath some unlimp lamp-post, wank-winking:
Come under the covers—come off!

THE SEMANTIC LIMERICK ACCORDING TO THE SHORTER OXFORD ENGLISH DICTIONARY (1933)

There existed an adult male person who had lived a relatively
short time, belonging or pertaining to St. John's*, who
desired to commit sodomy with the large web-footed
swimming birds of the genus *Cygnus* or subfamily *Cygninae*
of the family *Anatidae*, characterized by a long and
gracefully curved neck and a majestic motion when swimming.

So he moved into the presence of the person employed to
carry burdens, who declared: "Hold or possess as something
at your disposal my female child! The large web-footed
swimming-birds of the genus *Cygnus* or subfamily *Cygninae*
of the family *Anatidae*, characterized by a long and gracefully
curved neck and a majestic motion when swimming, are set
apart, specially retained for the Head, Fellows and Tutors
of the College!"

* A College of Cambridge University

THE SEMANTIC LIMERICK ACCORDING TO
DR. JOHNSON'S DICTIONARY (EDITION OF 1765)

There exifted a person, not a woman or a boy, being in the firft part of life, not old, of St. John's*, who wifhed to——— the large water-fowl, that have a long and very ftraight neck, and are very white, excepting when they are young (their legs and feet being black, as are their bills, which are like that of a goofe, but fomething rounder, and a little hooked at the lower ends, the two fides below their eyes being black and fhining like ebony).

In confequence of this he moved ftep by ftep to the one that had charge of the gate, who pronounced: "Poffefs and enjoy my female offspring! The large water-fowl, that have a long and very ftraight neck, and are very white, excepting when they are young (their legs and feet being black, as are their bills, which are like that of a goofe, but fomething rounder, and a little hooked at the lower ends, the two fides below their eyes being black and fhining like ebony) are kept in ftore, laid up for a future time, for the fake of the gentlemen with Spanish titles."

* A College of Cambridge University

Section 4

SONNET: DAFFODILS

Wordsworth really loved daffodils. He said they were flashers.
Certainly they must be the most exhibitionistic flowers
                                                    there are.
trumpeting their presence in yellow—by far the most
                                            visible colour.
I grant that after a long hard winter
it's warming to see snow-drops and crocuses in that iron earth
and the very first daffodils (what a cliché) seem a
                                            resurrection,
something it even seems appropriate to make a fuss about.
They look so perfect, though a bit self-conscious.

After a week or two, however, when Spring is established,
and everywhere you look there are oceans of daffodils
as arrogant as pop stars, they begin to seem ordinary.
You take them for granted. Like a love affair fading
they shrivel and go crinkly, papery and tired.
The Spring too (teenagers witness) has its own kind of
                                            boredom.

SONNET: BRIEF ENCOUNTER

Did we really make that journey to Northampton?
In pursuit of that coloured abortionist who did the first one?
He was very nice, you said, and had a cocktail cabinet,
and seemed clean. Two children, you said,
were quite enough for one lifetime—though I don't think any
of this did you much good, physically. I waited an hour
in the Station buffet. Then you came back, suffering
a state of shock, shivering. I bought you a whisky.

I did some shoe advertising once for a firm in Northampton.
Northampton is where they make shoes. They're fertility
                                                    symbols
(think of the old woman who lived in a shoe).
They're wombs and vaginas. "Something you put yout foot in"
I remember hearing a psychiatrist, once, say.
You felt very cold, in the train back to London.

SONNET: AT THE VILLA MADEIRA

So I sit here, in a comfortable chair, waiting
for the three bangs on the head with a wooden mallet
that will auction me, as it were, to Eternity.
I wear my long nightcap (nearly a bottle of whisky)
each night—and, later, a conventional Counsel
will call me a *mari complaisant*, something not very nice.
But really I neither know nor care what they get up to.
I was successful, and now I'm very depressed.

We get on well enough, with friendliness.
The times are bad (the times are always bad),
I sleep downstairs. We drink a bit—that's true.
I'm 67, she's 38, and he's 18.
These are all dangerous ages. Hypocrites in wigs
will make us ogres, who prove the power of love.

SONNET: WISE SIR BOWGENTLE

"Although he smiled, his eyes were fearful and his face had
aged much since Hawkmoon had last seen him—wise Sir
Bowgentle, the philosopher-poet."—Michael Moorcock, *The
Mad God's Amulet.*

He sounds a genuine phoney—to use an oldfashioned term.
It's not good for poets to fancy themselves as philosophers
(one reason why Auden was the best English poet since Pope).
Tennyson did himself a lot of harm by pondering;
the bromides of the Chorus are not the highspots of
                                        Greek Tragedy.
Politics too can bemuse the adept versifier.
Pound really believed he could have stopped Pearl Harbor
if he had gotten to the Japanese poets in time.

When the Bard, the Singer, is stuck there in front of the
                                        microphone
he makes mood music; he can't solve things for always—
all he can give is a certain amount of pleasure.
There still is an actual something we like to call Reality,
not much affected by our pretty words,
that mocks us with its Woody Woodpecker laugh.

SONNET: HOW LIFE TOO IS SENTIMENTAL

When our son was a few weeks old he had bronchial trouble
and picked up a cross-infection in the hospital
(salmonella typhimurium) through sluttish feeding—
but a hospital never admits it's responsible—
and was rushed away behind glass in an isolation ward,
at the point, it might be, of death. Our daughter,
eighteen months old, was just tall enough
to look into his empty cot and say: "Baby gone!"

A situation, an action and a speech
so tear-jerking that Dickens might have thought of them—
and indeed, in life, when we say "It couldn't happen!"
almost at once it happens. And the word "sentimental"
has come to mean exaggerated feeling.
It would have been hard to exaggerate *our* feelings then.

SONNET: GULLS

The old writers called somebody easily fooled "a gull".
Gulls never look credulous simpletons to me.
On the contrary they seem hard and rapacious
with beady eyes alert for the main chance,
more likely to do the conning than be conned,
while that horrible sex maniac's laugh they have
(one of the species is *cachinnans*, I believe)
is enough to upset anyone with a hangover.

"The probable sense was 'wailer' from its cry"
says my Shorter Oxford (Breton *goelaff*, to weep).
Doctor Johnson, of the tricky verb,
says "from *guiller*, to cheat, Old French",
the Shorter Oxford, cagey: "of doubtful origin".
This sounds more like the birds. *They* look real bastards.

SONNET: THE WOMANSMELL OF SEX

It's interesting how the sexual smell of women,
when they are excited by the touching of their lovers,
has never found its way into romantic literature
(nor, for that matter, into any other literature).
One poem by Donne. I can't think of much else.
The taboo must be very strong. Even pornography
describes visual and tactile but not the olfactory.
Some readers would go mad if it were even mentioned.

Of course, you can't describe a smell. Yet even hypocrites
would admit that for a man in love
this is an important factor in the physical attraction.
It should have, as it were, at least a footnote.
People don't like admitting that they're animals—
they turn their minds away from the fact and its proving.

SONNET: SHAKESPEARE'S UNIVERSALITY

In one sense Shakespeare's "universality" was accidental—
due to the fact that he wrote plays. When you have so many
                                       characters
you're bound to have so many views of human life.
Nobody can say "Why are all your poems about moles?"
or tell you you're very limited in your subject matter.
A playwright's material (unless it's outrageously slanted)
usually deals with a group of opinions; people can never say
"Of course this play is entirely autobiographical."

It's interesting that Shakespeare's Sonnets, which are
(I think we can't doubt) completely based on his life,
are by a long way his least satisfactory verse.
It's better for a writer, in most cases, to get out and about.
If he gets stuck in his own psyche for too long
he bores everybody—and that includes himself.

SONNET: AFTERWARDS

When I am gone, the whole satirical setup
will carry on as before—into the foreseeable future
the world will fill itself like a basin of water
with all the archetypes. The lonely, the mother-fixated,
the psychopaths, the deviants. The big superstitious religions
will enrol from birth their thousands and tens of thousands.
The smug, the respected, the cheer-leaders, the purse-proud.
People will still believe it is right to kill people.

I shall have done little enough to improve the cosmos—
my political influence nil, my personal kindness
only a drop in an ocean where already the children
are born who will commit the next century's murders,
my love so transient it's pathetic. They'll say (if I'm lucky):
He wrote some silly poems, and some of them were funny.